Story Writing

BY KAREN KELLAHER

SCHOLASTIC
PROFESSIONAL BOOKS

NEW YORK • TORONTO • LONDON • AUCKLAND • SYDNEY
MEXICO CITY • NEW DELHI • HONG KONG • BUENOS AIRES

To Colin,

my inspiration

Front cover and interior design by Kathy Massaro
Cover art by Jon Buller
Interior art by Michael Moran
Poster art by Laura Cornell

ISBN: 0-439-28843-6
Copyright © 2002 by Karen Kellaher
Published by Scholastic Inc.
All rights reserved.
Printed in the U.S.A.

1 2 3 4 5 6 7 8 9 10   40   09 08 07 06 05 04 03 02

Contents

Introduction 4

   About This Series 4

   About This Book 4

   Correlations With the Language Arts Standards .. 5

   Teaching With the Poster:

     Recipe for Good Writing—Stories That Sizzle .. 5

CHAPTER 1

Getting Started:
Setting the Stage for Writing 7

Strategy 1: Sharing Samples of Various Genres .. 7

   Visiting the Genres 8

Strategy 2: Writing Collaborative Stories 9

* Strategy 3: Using Pictures to Spark Creativity .. 10

* Strategy 4: Keeping Idea Notebooks 12

CHAPTER 2

Exploring Story Elements 14

Exploring Setting

   * Set-the Scene Board Game 15

   * Create Setting Postcards 16

Exploring Character Development

   * Create a Character Photo Frame 20

   * Character-Speech Spinner 21

Exploring Plot

   * Lift-the-Flap Plot Square 25

   * Problem-Solution Flowchart 26

   * Character-Plot-Setting Trifold 26

Exploring Point of View

   * *The Tortoise and the Hare*
     Point-of-View Mini-Book 31

Exploring Dialogue

   * What Did They Say? 35

Exploring Word Choice and Story Organization

   * Be Specific! Story Puzzle 37

CHAPTER 3

Bringing Stories to Life:
Exploring Story Genres 39

   * I'm the Star of the Story
   Writing Skills: Exploring Personal Narratives 39

   * Be a Mythmaker
   Writing Skills: Exploring Myths 45

   * Adventure Awaits
   Writing Skills: Exploring Adventures 48

   * Crack the Case!
   Writing Skills: Exploring Mysteries 52

Additional Ideas for Exploring
Different Genres 55

   * Historical Fiction 55

   Tall Tales 55

   * Fantasy and Fairy Tales 56

   Humor 57

CHAPTER 4

Wrapping Up Stories: Suggestions for
Editing, Publishing, and Assessing 60

   Suggestions for Editing, Publishing,
     and Assessing Stories 60

     STUDENT CHECKLIST: Editing My Story 62

     STUDENT CHECKLIST: Editing Symbols 63

     TEACHER RUBRIC: Assessing Student Stories 64

* INCLUDES REPRODUCIBLE KIDS' PAGE(S)

Introduction

ABOUT THIS SERIES:
Building Skills in Writing

Most of us write every day. We write when we make a grocery list, when we e-mail a faraway friend, and when we prepare our lesson plans. But rarely do we stop to think about what we're really doing when we put pen to paper or fingers to keyboard. What, exactly, is writing?

Educator Donald Murray once said that writing is the act of using language to "discover meaning in experience and communicate it."* For me, this definition sums up the most important aspects of the writing process. First, it reminds us that writing is rooted in personal experience. Without experience, we have no meaning to communicate. Second, Murray's definition underscores the fact that writing always has a purpose and an audience. The very idea of "communicating" meaning implies that there is someone to receive the message, even if that audience is simply oneself at a later moment in time.

As teachers of emergent writers, you have an exciting job—to help bring this definition to life for your students. This series, *Building Skills in Writing*, is designed to assist you in this role. Each of the three books—*Story Writing, Report Writing,* and *Responding to Literature*—features lessons, strategies, activities, reproducibles, teaching tips, rubrics, and checklists to help your students write for a specific purpose and audience. Each addresses all stages of the writing process, from prewriting through publishing and assessment.

ABOUT THIS BOOK:
Story Writing

Writing original stories offers students a sense of accomplishment and empowerment that few other school experiences can match. Because stories spring from the imagination, putting them on paper is like sharing a part of ourselves. Students' confidence blooms as they transform a grain of an idea that exists only in their mind into a real, printed story that entertains others. The process—and the pride on students' faces when they "publish" a piece—are purely magical.

At the same time, some children are intimidated by the idea of writing stories. Coming up with a good idea and then developing that idea can feel like enormous undertakings (even to professional authors!). This book will help you

* *Learning by Teaching: Selected Articles on Writing and Teaching.* Upper Montclair, New Jersey: Boynton/Cook, 1982, p. 10

ease those writing jitters in two important ways: first, by introducing story writing as an exciting and enjoyable process that can be approached in small steps, and second, by providing plenty of opportunities for students to practice, practice, practice!

Specifically, this book will help you teach students to:

◎ develop a setting and characters.

◎ create a plot with a central conflict and satisfying resolution.

◎ organize a story in a way that is interesting to the reader.

◎ use sensory details and concrete language to develop the story.

◎ edit for grammar, punctuation, spelling, and capitalization.

◎ use dialogue, suspense, and other strategies to move the plot along.

◎ evaluate their own and others' stories.

TEACHING WITH THE POSTER:
Recipe for Good Writing—Stories That Sizzle

Don't miss "Recipe for Good Writing: Stories That Sizzle," the full-color poster that came with this book. Designed to look like a recipe card, the poster invites students to think of writing stories as a delicious process. With the right main ingredients—characters, setting, plot, conflict—and "seasonings" to taste, your students can concoct stories to savor!

Display the poster and refer to it frequently as you teach the story-writing process. Distribute smaller copies of the poster for children to use as learning place mats (see page 6). Students can tape the mini-posters to their desks or insert them in binders for homework help. For best results, laminate the place mats or paste them onto sheets of construction paper.

Correlations With the Language Arts Standards

The activities in this book are aligned with the following language arts standards outlined by the Mid-Continent Regional Educational Laboratory (MCREL), an organization that collects and synthesizes noteworthy national and state K–12 curriculum standards.

◎ Writes narrative accounts, including stories:
  ● develops characters, setting, and plot
  ● includes a beginning, middle, and ending
  ● sequences events
  ● uses concrete sensory details

◎ Uses prewriting strategies such as graphic organizers and note-taking to plan written work

◎ Uses strategies to draft, organize and revise written work
  ● Elaborates on a central idea
  ● Writes with attention to word choice and audience

◎ Uses strategies to edit and publish written work

◎ Evaluates own and others' writing

Source: *A Compendium of Standards and Benchmarks for K–12 Education* (Mid-Continent Regional Educational Laboratory, 1995).

Stories That Sizzle

Recipe for Good Writing

Ingredients:

- **Characters**
- **Setting**
- **Plot** (including a **good beginning, middle, and ending**)
- **Title**

Directions:

1 Prepare interesting **characters**. You should have at least one main character.

2 Whip up a **setting**, or place and time where your story will take place.

3 Brainstorm what will happen in your story. This is the **plot**.

4 Cook up a **beginning** that catches the reader's attention.

5 Mix in some suspense! Tell what happens leading up to the main event.

6 Add the main event. It's the problem that happens in the **middle** of the story. Use a lot of details! Don't forget to tell what the main character is thinking or feeling.

7 Stir up a great **ending**. It tells how the problem is fixed.

8 Top the story off with a terrific **title**.

9 Before serving, remove any mistakes in grammar and spelling. Ask a partner to sample your story and help you find ways to spice it up.

Serving Suggestion:

Publish your story! Make a cover and bind the pages together with staples or string. Share it with friends.

Getting Started: Setting the Stage for Writing

Just as a chef starts off by choosing a recipe and gathering the necessary ingredients, a writer begins with a nugget of an idea and a sense of what makes a story work. In this section you'll find strategies for introducing story writing in your classroom and for helping students generate all-star story ideas.

STRATEGY 1:
Sharing Samples of Various Genres

You're probably already preparing students for story writing in an important way—by reading to them on a regular basis. Reading aloud exposes students to various genres of literature (mysteries, fairy tales, and so on) and helps them learn to recognize the characteristics of effective writing. As you teach students to write stories of their own, be sure to choose read-aloud books from various genres. Consult the list that follows for a few examples from each genre that I think are especially suitable for second- and third-graders. If you can, allow an extra five to ten minutes for each read-aloud period to discuss what makes each type of book interesting and unique. Later, when students try their own hand at each genre, they will have tried-and-true models to use.

Let students sharpen their story-writing skills by interacting with the stories you read aloud. For example, students might:

◎ write a new ending for a familiar story.

◎ retell a story from the point of view of a different character.

◎ write original stories featuring beloved characters from popular book series, such as Arthur (from the series by Marc Brown) or Alexander (who stars in several books by Judith Viorst).

◎ draw and describe the settings of the books you read together.

For many other interesting ways to have students respond to stories, check out the companion volume to this book, *Building Skills in Writing: Responding to Literature.*

Visiting the Genres

A **personal narrative** shares an event from the author's/narrator's life. Examples:

◎ *Owl Moon*, by Jane Yolen (Putnam, 1987). The narrator and her father go owl-watching on a beautiful night.

◎ *The Wednesday Surprise*, by Eve Bunting (Houghton Mifflin, 1990). Anna, the narrator, teaches her grandmother to read.

A **mystery** story has a puzzling situation, someone trying to solve the mystery, and a resolution. Examples:

◎ *The Mystery of the Missing Red Mitten*, by Steven Kellogg (Econo-Clad Books, 1999). Annie must find her mitten—the fifth one she's lost this year!

◎ *Detective Dinosaur*, by James Skofield (HarperCollins, 1998). A bumbling sleuth solves three cases.

A **fantasy** story is not based in reality. It presents people, places, events, or things that could exist only in a person's imagination. Fairy tales are one type of fantasy story. Examples:

◎ *Lon Po Po: A Red Riding Hood Story From China*, by Ed Young (Philomel Books, 1989). This version of the classic fairy tale is from China.

◎ *The Elves and the Shoemaker*, by the Brothers Grimm (Many publishers). Elves step in at night to help an old shoemaker finish his work.

A **myth** or **folktale** is a story people made up to explain why something is so. It is not a true story. Examples:

◎ *Why Mosquitoes Buzz in People's Ears*, retold by Verna Aardema (Penguin, 1975). This African "why" story is a great model for students to follow.

◎ *Thirteen Moons on Turtle's Back: A Native American Year of Moons*, by Joseph Bruchac (Putnam, 1997). This story recounts the legend behind each moon of the year.

An **adventure** is a story about an exciting experience. Examples:

◎ *Afternoon on the Amazon*, by Mary Pope Osbourne (Magic Tree House Series, Random House, 1995). The characters meet giant ants, hungry crocodiles, and more.

◎ *Dandelions*, by Eve Bunting (Harcourt, 1995). Zoe and her family make a new home in the rugged Nebraska territory.

A **humorous story** is meant to make the reader laugh. Examples:

◎ *Alexander and the Terrible, Horrible, No Good, Very Bad Day*, by Judith Viorst (Simon & Schuster, 1976). Alexander's day starts with chewing gum in his hair and only gets worse.

◎ *Dog Breath*, by Dav Pilkey (Blue Sky Press, 1994). Halitosis the dog earns his keep by scaring away burglars—the smelly way.

Historical fiction is set in the past and weaves details about the time and place into the story. Characters may be fictional or real. Examples:

◎ *In America*, by Marissa Moss (Dutton, 1994). Walter's grandfather tells the story of when he immigrated to America from Lithuania.

◎ *Jumping the Broom*, by Courtni C. Wright (Holiday House, 1994). Eight-year-old Lettie, a slave girl, enjoys her sister's wedding day.

A **tall tale** is a story that uses exaggeration. The characters and plots in tall tales may be based in truth, but they are exaggerated to make the story larger than life. Examples:

◎ *Paul Bunyan*, by Steven Kellogg (William Morrow & Co., 1985). The story of the world's biggest lumberjack.

◎ *John Henry*, by Julius Lester (Dial, 1994). An entertaining story about a contest between an American hero and a steam engine. Based on an African-American folk ballad.

STRATEGY 2:

Writing Collaborative Stories

Many students do not automatically see themselves as writers. Here's a case in point: At a recent family function, I found myself at the "kids' end" of the restaurant table, happily entertaining both my own young children and my nephews, one of whom was just completing second grade. When the antics at our end of the table began attracting attention from nearby diners, I suggested that we make up a story together. "I can't," replied my nephew, who is quite smart and imaginative. "I don't know how to do that." But when I began throwing out possible titles for the story (*The Ziti From Mars, Michael's Lost Tooth*, and so on), my nephew excitedly threw himself into the activity. After we had all collaborated on one zany tale, he came up with another original story on his own. His story, *Stinky: The Dog Who Wouldn't Take a Bath*, kept us laughing all the way through dessert!

As this experience suggests, some reluctant writers may simply need a catalyst to help them realize that story writing is not so scary. One fun way to ease students into story writing is to create a class collaborative story. Here's how:

1 Start off with an open-ended, interesting sentence, such as "Once there was a worm named Gertie who was terribly afraid of _____."

2 Let a student volunteer fill in the blank. Then go around the classroom asking each student to add one or two sentences.

3 From time to time, take another turn as narrator and add a sentence that will help students move the tale along—for example, "Finally, Gertie thought of a solution to her embarrassing problem."

4 Be sure to record the story so that students can edit it and enjoy it again and again. You can either jot it down on chart paper as students compose the story or use a tape recorder and transcribe the story onto paper at your convenience.

Write On!

Stuck for a collaborative story starter? Try one of these:

◎ I never believed that there was life in outer space. Then, one day last summer, I learned the amazing truth. It all started when _____...

◎ Once upon a time, a beautiful princess roamed the land in search of a magic _____...

◎ One rainy Saturday I was exploring the attic of our house when I spotted something really strange. It was a _____...

STRATEGY 3: **Using Pictures to Spark Creativity**

(Use with the reproducible below and Kids' Page 11.)

Do your students sometimes complain that they can't think of anything to write about? Use picture flash cards to inspire creativity. Hunt for humorous or interesting photographs in magazines, newspapers, even your own family scrapbook. (See page 11 for two Picture-Prompt photos to help you get started.) Once a week, share a photo with the class. Invite students to summarize what they think is happening in the picture, using the Picture-Prompt Response Card below.

This activity is designed to let students flex their imaginative muscles in short writing sessions. Students need not worry about writing a full story to go with each picture, but they may wish to save their favorite response cards and expand them into complete stories at a later date. By introducing at least one photograph each week, you'll get students accustomed to writing on a regular basis.

Picture-Prompt Response Card

1. Who or what is in this picture? Give each character a name and describe him or her.

_____

_____

2. Where is this scene taking place?

_____

_____

3. What's going on in the picture? Use your imagination!

_____

_____

4. What might have happened just before this photo was snapped?

_____

_____

5. What will happen next?

_____

_____

AP Photo/Salt Lake Tribune/Lynn R. Johnson

The Image Bank/Getty Images

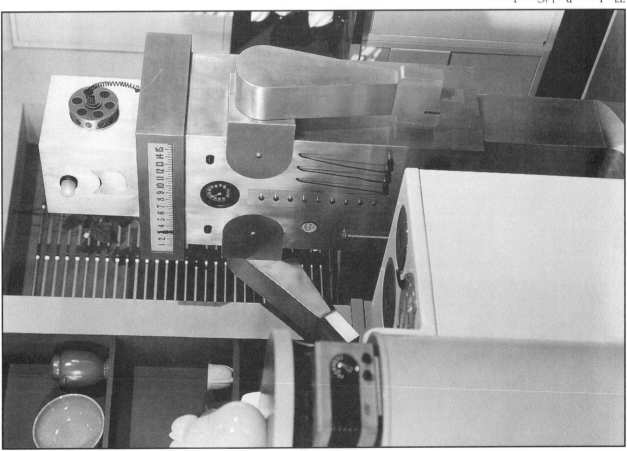

STRATEGY 4:

Keeping Idea Notebooks

(Use with Kids' Page 13.)

One irony I've learned about story writing is that when you sit down to draft a tale, generating ideas can be like squeezing water from a stone. At virtually any other time—whether you're feeding ducks in the park or shopping for new shoes—ideas can bombard you from all directions! Many professional authors accept this as a funny quirk of the writing process and use it to their advantage by carrying around special idea notebooks. They use the notebooks to record ideas in all forms—plot concepts, illustrations of settings, potential story titles, names for new characters, and so on. Later, a few of those ideas just might turn into full-fledged stories.

Have students keep idea notebooks of their own so that no good idea gets lost in the shuffle. If students already keep daily journals, you might simply designate a section of the journal for story ideas. (Use a sticky note or colored tab to show where this special section begins.) Otherwise, have each child get a notebook or binder to use specifically for story brainstorming.

Encourage students to keep their idea notebooks with them whenever practical. When students finish work early or have a spare minute or two, allow them to write and/or draw in their idea notebooks. Students may also wish to paste or tape some of their Picture-Prompt Response Cards (see strategy 3, page 10) in their notebooks. When it's time to select a story idea and begin writing, students can refer to their notebooks for inspiration. If you notice that a student is not able to generate an idea for a story, ask if you might review his or her notebook together. Point out ways for some of the child's written or illustrated ideas to be fleshed out into stories.

If students are still stuck for inspiration, distribute copies of the Authors' Idea Zone reproducible on page 13. The children's authors named on the checklist have been generous enough to share their advice with interviewers over the years. These tips are paraphrased from individual author Web sites and from *The Big Book of Picture-Book Authors & Illustrators* (Scholastic, 2001). Have students tape the checklist to the inside covers of their idea notebooks for ready-to-go inspiration.

Source: Adapted from individual author Web sites and *The Big Book of Picture-Book Authors & Illustrators,* by James Preller (Scholastic, 2001).

Building Skills in Writing: Story Writing   Scholastic Professional Books

Authors' Idea Zone

Here's how some famous authors come up with their best ideas. How many of these tips have you tried?

○ Turn off the TV. For at least one day, go without TV. Find someplace where you can be alone with your thoughts.

—**Shonto Begay**, author of *The Mud Pony*

○ Be a sponge. Pay attention to the ordinary things happening all around you. Some small detail might make you think of a great story.

—**Marc Brown**, author of *Arthur*

○ Hunt for family stories. Ask older relatives questions about what things were like when they were growing up.

—**Gloria Houston**, author of *My Great-Aunt Arizona*

○ Turn a newspaper article into a story. Read the local newspaper and choose an article about a real-life event. Now imagine yourself at the center of the news event. Think about how you would tell the story and what might happen next.

—**Eve Bunting**, author of *How Many Days to America?*

○ Use your memory. Remember something interesting or special that has happened to you. Write it down.

—**Allen Say**, author of *Grandfather's Journey*

○ Write about a time you had strong feelings about something— for example, a time you felt very mad, happy, sad, nervous, or afraid.

—**Charlotte Zolotow**, author of *If You Listen*

2

Exploring Story Elements

Whew! Now that you've helped your students brainstorm loads of exciting ideas, you're ready for a SPA treatment. No, I don't mean a day of pampering at an all-star resort (although you may well be ready for one of those, too!). This SPA treatment stands for Show, Practice, and Apply, and it's a fun and effective way to introduce students to the basic elements of a good story. These elements include setting, characters, plot, point of view, organization, dialogue, and effective word choice. To use the SPA treatment in your classroom:

◎ **Show** students how real authors incorporate these story elements into their stories by calling attention to examples of the effective use of the elements in books you read together. For a short list of recommended books, see page 8. For a lengthier list, consult the companion volume to this book, *Building Skills in Writing: Responding to Literature.*

◎ Have students **practice** using the story elements by working on the activities and reproducibles in this chapter. The chapter is divided into the following sections: Exploring Setting, Exploring Character Development, Exploring Plot, Exploring Point of View, Exploring Dialogue, and Exploring Word Choice and Story Organization. Each section includes reproducible activities that will help students learn about that story element in creative ways.

◎ Encourage students to **apply** all of the story elements to their own writing. In chapter 3 you'll find writing activities to share with students.

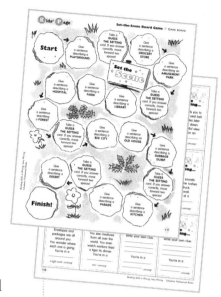

Exploring Setting

Set-the-Scene Board Game

(Use with Kids' Pages 17 and 18.)

The *setting* is the place and time in which a story takes place. In this board-game activity for two to four players, students learn to describe settings using vivid, concrete language. Here's how to play (you can make copies of the directions for students):

How to Play:

1 Give each group a copy of the game board and the cards. Each group will also need a coin.

2 Have each player choose a game marker to move around the board. No two markers should be exactly the same.

3 Put the cards facedown in a pile near the game board. Use the blank cards to create your own clues about local settings, if desired.

4 Have the players use a fair method to determine who will go first. Player 1 flips the coin. If the coin lands heads up, the player moves two spaces. If the coin lands heads down, the player moves one space.

5 If player 1 lands on a space with the name of a setting, he or she must give one sentence that describes that setting. (IMPORTANT RULE: If another player later lands on the same setting, he or she cannot repeat the same idea.)

6 If player 1 lands on a GUESS THE SETTING space, he or she must identify a setting from one of the GUESS THE SETTING cards. The player to his or her left should take a card and read aloud the clue. If player 1 can name the setting, he or she moves forward one space.

7 The next player to take a turn is the student sitting to the left of player 1. The winner is the first player to reach the finish line.

Materials

- copies of Kids' Pages 17 and 18 for each playing group
- scissors
- coins
- game markers (buttons, colored paper clips, or other small items)

Materials

- copy of Kids' Page 19 for each student
- scissors
- glue sticks

It's About Time

Setting is not just about where the story happens; it also includes when the tale occurs. For example, a piece of historical fiction might have seventeenth-century colonial America as its setting. A sci-fi story might take place in the year 2512. As students become more familiar with the idea of setting, encourage them to try writing stories that happen in the past or future. Consider revisiting the postcard activity on this page, this time with the additional instruction that the setting must be a time other than the present.

Create Setting Postcards

(Use with Kids' Page 19.)

Looking for a way to help students immerse themselves in their stories? Invite them to make postcards that feature their story setting! Postcards are an exciting way to explore setting because they communicate the most important and interesting aspects of a locale in very few words. To try this activity in your classroom, distribute copies of the Setting Postcards reproducible on page 19 and ask students to imagine one of their favorite places in the world. It may be an exotic location where they once vacationed, a special spot in their own home, or even someplace they've never been but have imagined many times. Once each student has settled on a locale, do the following:

1 Have students cut out the postcard along the dotted lines and fold it in half along the solid line. Then, direct them to use a very thin layer of glue to secure the fold. Let dry.

2 Invite students to draw their settings on the "Greetings from…" side of the postcard.

3 On the text side of the postcard, instruct students to write a detailed description of their setting. They should write as if they are describing the place to someone who has never seen it. Examples of details might include:

- ◎ things they see, hear, and smell.
- ◎ descriptions of the climate or weather.
- ◎ descriptions of special activities that take place in the setting.

If you wish, have students address their postcards to each other or to family members. (Many students will find it helpful to have a specific reader in mind for their writing.)

4 Some students may wish to use their setting postcards as starting points for stories. Simply encourage students to remember something interesting that happened to them there—or something interesting that *could* happen there.

Start

Give a sentence describing a **PLAYGROUND**.

Take a **GUESS THE SETTING** card. If you answer correctly, move forward two spaces!

Give a sentence describing a **GROCERY STORE**.

Give a sentence describing an **AMUSEMENT PARK**.

Set the Scene

Give a sentence describing a **HOSPITAL**.

Give a sentence describing a **FARM**.

Give a sentence describing a **LIBRARY**.

Take a **GUESS THE SETTING** card. If you answer correctly, move forward two spaces!

Give a sentence describing a **FOREST**.

Take a **GUESS THE SETTING** card. If you answer correctly, move forward two spaces!

Give a sentence describing a **BIG CITY**.

Give a sentence describing an **OLD HOUSE**.

Give a sentence describing a **GARBAGE DUMP**.

Give a sentence describing a **DESERT**.

Take a **GUESS THE SETTING** card. If you answer correctly, move forward two spaces!

Take a **GUESS THE SETTING** card. If you answer correctly, move forward two spaces!

Finish!

Give a sentence describing a **PARADE**.

Give a sentence describing a **KITCHEN**.

Building Skills in Writing: Story Writing
Scholastic Professional Books

GUESS the Setting...

The smell of hot dogs fills the air. You hear a loud crack and people cheering. You're at a

_____ .

Answer: baseball game

GUESS the Setting...

Children play in the waves and build castles. Gulls fly overhead. You're at the

_____ .

Answer: beach

GUESS the Setting...

Kids carry trays piled high with burgers and green beans. You can't wait to get outside to play. You're in the

_____ .

Answer: cafeteria

GUESS the Setting...

A voice tells you to fasten your seat belt. Ten minutes later you look down at a beautiful view. You're on an

_____ .

Answer: airplane

GUESS the Setting...

You squeeze your eyes shut as you hear the sound of the drill. "Open wide," a voice says. You're at the

_____ .

Answer: dentist's office

GUESS the Setting...

It's a fall morning. You see rows of trees loaded with round, ripe fruit. Red, green, or yellow…you can't decide which to pick first. You're in an

_____ .

Answer: apple orchard

GUESS the Setting...

A young man smiles and asks if you are ready to order. Your stomach is growling. You're in a

_____ .

Answer: restaurant

GUESS the Setting...

An alarm sounds and everyone rushes to the truck. Sirens wail. You're at a

_____ .

Answer: firehouse

GUESS the Setting...

Envelopes and packages are all around you. You wonder where each one is going. You're in a

_____ .

Answer: post office

GUESS the Setting...

You see creatures from all over the world. You even watch workers feed a tiger its dinner. You're in a

_____ .

Answer: zoo

GUESS the Setting...

Write your own clue:

_____

_____

_____

You're in a

_____ .

Answer:

GUESS the Setting...

Write your own clue:

_____

_____

_____

You're in a

_____ .

Answer:

Setting Postcards

Postcard Front

Greetings from

!

_____
(your setting)

Draw a picture of your setting.

Fold ◄   ► **Fold**

(your name)
Signed, _____

_____

_____

_____

_____

_____

_____

This place is so special!

Dear _____,

Send to:

_____

_____

_____

Postcard Back

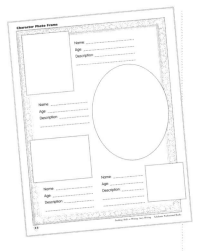

Materials

- copy of Kids' Page 22 for each student
- 9- by 12-inch sheet of construction paper, one sheet per student
- scissors
- glue sticks

Create a Character Photo Frame

(Use with Kids' Page 22.)

Have you ever shared a family photo album with an acquaintance who does not know your loved ones very well? You probably found yourself explaining with each picture, "This is my Uncle Frank. He loves playing practical jokes on everyone," or "That's my good friend Christina. We've known each other since we were 6." For me, that's what the early stages of character development feel like. As I create characters in my mind, I mull over the individual's unique physical and personality traits as well as the ties that bind that character to the rest of the cast (Will this guy be the main character's cousin or brother? Will my heroine be shy or outgoing?). At this stage I am meeting my characters for the first time; I want to be sure I get to know them rather well before I introduce them to my readers.

In this activity your students get a chance to try this character-development technique by filling in a mock photo frame with as many as four story characters. (If students want to create more than four characters, they can use multiple copies of the reproducible.) This activity works best once students have a solid idea for a story. Here's what to do:

1 If possible, bring in a photo frame from home that holds multiple pictures. Tell the class a bit about each person pictured. (Your students will get a huge kick out of hearing about the people in your life!) Then explain that students will be making a similar frame for the characters in their stories.

2 Distribute the Character Photo Frame reproducible on page 22. Instruct students to draw their story characters in the photo frames. I recommend using the large oval in the center for the narrator/main character.

3 On the lines next to each frame, have students write a bit about each character. Descriptions should include name and age and might also cover the character's personality, interests, hobbies, and relationship to the main character. You might put several examples on the board to give students some models to follow. For example:

Nina
Age 7
Supersmart
Loves horses and solving mysteries

Jillian (also known as Jilly)
Age 10
Nina's big sister
Very bossy!

4 Have students cut out their frames along the outer dotted lines and glue their completed reproducibles onto slightly larger pieces of colored paper. This will give the appearance of real photo frames.

Character-Speech Spinner

(Use with Kids' Pages 23 and 24.)

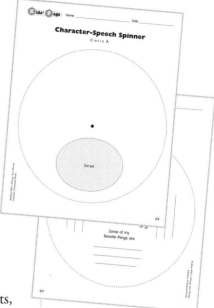

Another fun way to develop characters for a story is to imagine how the characters might answer if you were to ask them questions about themselves. In this activity, students will create a face-shaped spinner for their main characters. As the student rotates the spinner, the featured character gets a chance to share some details about himself or herself. To make the spinners:

1 Have students cut out the two pieces that make up the Character-Speech spinner—the face template (circle A) and the text circle (circle B).

2 Help students carefully cut out the oval mouth shape from circle A. This will be the window in which questions and answers appear. For best results, help each student carefully poke one point of the scissors through the paper to begin to cut.

3 Invite students to think about how their character would complete the statements on circle B, and then fill in the answers on the circle.

4 Instruct students to put circle A on top of circle B and secure a brass fastener through the center of the two circles. Students can then decorate the front of the spinner to look like the character described. They can use crayons or markers to color the face and even glue yarn or construction paper onto the spinner for hair and eyes. To read and share the spinners, students simply turn the top circle to expose each frame.

5 If desired, have students repeat steps 1 through 4 for each character in their stories. Even after their stories have been completed, students will enjoy sharing their manipulatives with friends and family.

Materials

- copies of Kids' Pages 23 and 24 for each student
- scissors
- brass fasteners
- crayons or markers
- yarn, construction paper, googly-eyes, and other craft materials
- glue

Character Photo Frame

Name: _____

Age: _____

Description: _____

_____

Name: _____

Age: _____

Description: _____

_____

Name: _____

Age: _____

Description: _____

_____

Name: _____

Age: _____

Description: _____

_____

Name _____ Date _____

Character-Speech Spinner

CIRCLE A

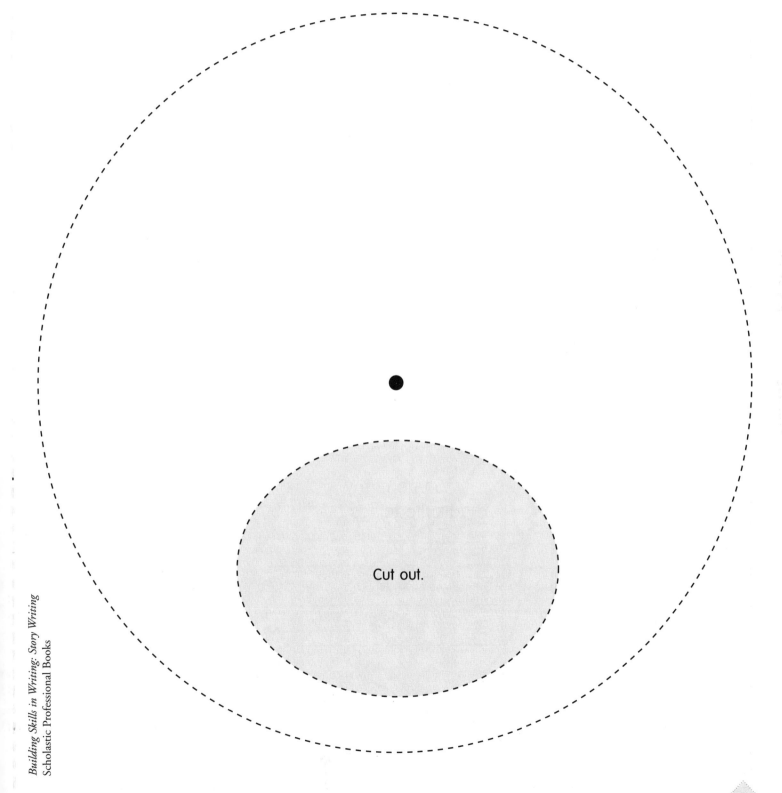

Cut out.

Building Skills in Writing: Story Writing
Scholastic Professional Books

Character-Speech Spinner

CIRCLE B

_____

and I am

Hi! My name is

One thing
I'm good at is

Some of my least
favorite things are

Some of my
favorite things are

_____

_____

_____

Building Skills in Writing: Story Writing
Scholastic Professional Books

Exploring Plot

Lift-the-Flap Plot Square

(Use with Kids' Pages 27 and 28.)

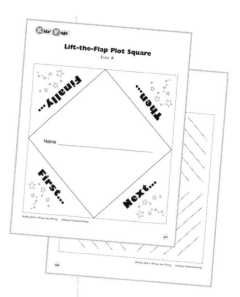

Plot is one of the most important elements of a good story. After all, what good is a fascinating character if he or she never *does* anything? Explain to students that plot is what happens in a story. Very often the plot revolves around a problem, or conflict, and a solution to that problem.

In this activity students make fun manipulatives to help them plan the plot sequence of their stories. Before beginning, make sure each student has an idea for a story. To construct the plot squares:

1 Make a double-sided copy of pages 27 and 28 for each student.

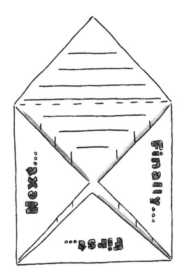

2 Have students cut out the square along the outer dotted lines and then fold each of the four corners on side B in along the solid lines. They should now have a square with four triangular-shaped flaps on top.

Materials

- double-sided copy of Kids' Pages 27 and 28 for each student
- scissors
- posterboard
- glue stick

3 Explain that students can follow the words on the flaps to put the events in their stories in order. Students should lift the flaps one by one—First, Next, Then, and Finally. Under each flap, they should describe that segment of their plot. Share this example with students, or make up one of your own:

First... Baxter finds a $20 bill in the library.

Next... Baxter sees an ad for an action figure and decides to buy it with the money.

Then... Baxter learns that the librarian has lost $20. He doesn't know what to do.

Finally... Baxter returns the money to the librarian. Later he gets the toy he wants for his birthday!

4 To help your class's plot squares hold up over time, glue the underside of the square to a piece of posterboard.

Materials

● copy of Kids'
Page 29 for each
student

Problem-Solution Flowchart

(Use with Kids' Page 29.)

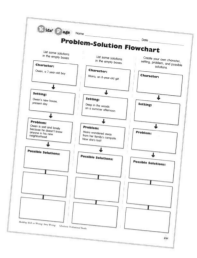

One challenge of concocting a captivating plot is
to think up a conflict that a specific character in a
specific setting would be likely to face. Another
challenge is to come up with a resolution to the
problem that's believable yet interesting. In this
activity students practice both of these aspects of
plot development. In the first two exercises on
the Problem-Solution Flowchart on page 29, we
provide the character, setting, and problem, and
your students list possible solutions. In the last exercise students develop
all four of the elements on their own—character, setting, problem, and solution.
Once they have done so, they are well on their way to a solid story!

Point out to students that it's useful to think of several potential solutions to a
problem before settling on one. Story resolutions, or endings, can be happy, sad,
expected, surprising, and many things in between.

Materials

● copy of Kids'
Page 30 for
each student
● scissors
● tape or glue
sticks

Character-Plot-Setting Trifold

(Use with Kids' Page 30.)

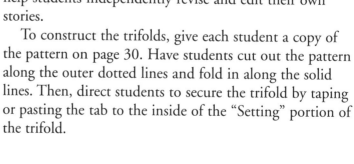

At this point, your students have explored the three
most basic elements of a good story: character,
setting, and plot. Before moving on to other aspects
of story writing, have students create Character-Plot-
Setting trifolds with ready-to-use tips on developing
these three vital story
elements. Students can
decorate their trifolds and display them on
their desks at writing time. The trifolds are designed to
help students independently revise and edit their own
stories.

To construct the trifolds, give each student a copy of
the pattern on page 30. Have students cut out the pattern
along the outer dotted lines and fold in along the solid
lines. Then, direct students to secure the trifold by taping
or pasting the tab to the inside of the "Setting" portion of
the trifold.

Lift-the-Flap Plot Square

SIDE A

Finally...

Then...

Name _____

First...

Next...

Lift-the-Flap Plot Square

SIDE B

Name _____   Date _____

Problem-Solution Flowchart

| List some solutions in the empty boxes. | List some solutions in the empty boxes. | Create your own character, setting, problem, and possible solutions. |

Character:
Owen, a 7-year-old boy

Setting:
Owen's new house, present day

Problem:
Owen is sad and lonely because he doesn't know anyone in his new neighborhood.

Possible Solutions:

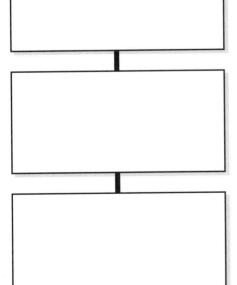

Character:
Moira, an 8-year-old girl

Setting:
Deep in the woods on a summer afternoon

Problem:
Moira wandered away from her family's campsite. Now she's lost!

Possible Solutions:

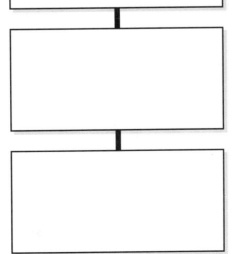

Character:

Setting:

Problem:

Possible Solutions:

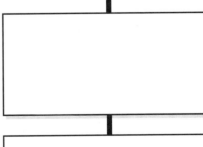

Plot

- Plot is what happens in your story.

- Make sure your story plot has a beginning, middle, and ending.

- In the beginning, build up to a problem.

- In the middle, make your character face a problem.

- In the ending, show how the problem was solved.

Character

- Characters are the people or animals in your story.

- Have at least one main character. Introduce him or her at the beginning. You can introduce other characters whenever you want.

- Describe how your characters look and act.

- Show, don't just tell! Don't just say a character is smart or shy—give examples that show these qualities to the reader.

- Give each character a name that suits him or her.

Setting

- Setting is where and when the story takes place.

- Describe your setting near the beginning of your story.

- Pretend you're describing the setting to someone who has never been there.

- Use your senses! Tell what your character sees, hears, feels, tastes, or smells in the setting.

Building Skills in Writing: Story Writing Scholastic Professional Books

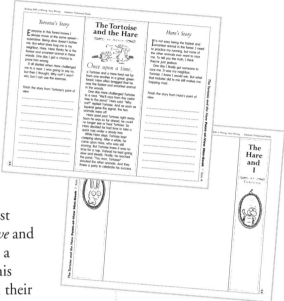

Exploring Point of View

The Tortoise and the Hare Point-of-View Mini-Book

(Use with Kids' Pages 33 and 34.)

Explain to students that point of view is the perspective from which a story is written. To find the point of view of a story, students should ask, "Who is telling the story?" Many stories are told from the first-person point of view. A story written in the first person uses the personal pronouns *I* and *me* (or, less frequently, *we* and *us*). That's because the narrator, or person telling the story, is also a character in the story. Students who choose to tell a story from this vantage point can have fun thinking about who will be the "I" in their story. For example, a student writing an updated version of *Goldilocks and the Three Bears* could tell the story from the perspective of Goldilocks, one of the bears, or even a squirrel who witnessed the whole fiasco!

Other stories are written from a third-person point of view. In these, the narrator is not a character in the story but an outsider looking in. Although the focus of the story is probably on one character, that character is not personally telling the story.

It's important for students to realize that they can use any point of view they wish for their stories. In fact, by experimenting with different points of view, they may make their writing more creative and fun.

In this mini-book activity students will explore the classic story of *The Tortoise and the Hare* from three different points of view—an outside observer (Aesop, the original story creator), the Tortoise, and, finally, the Hare. Students will first read the third-person account, then retell the story from the two animals' perspectives. Here's what to do:

Materials

- double-sided copy of Kids' Pages 33 and 34 for each student
- scissors

1. Make a double-sided copy of pages 33 and 34 for each student. Have students cut out the pattern along the outer dotted lines and then place it in front of them with the story side (side A) facing up.

2. Then, instruct students to fold the right and left edges of the page in toward the center (use the solid lines on side B as a guide). They will now see three titles along the top: *The Hare and I*, by Tortoise (at left); *The Tortoise and the Hare* (at center); and *That Terrible Tortoise*, by Hare (at right).

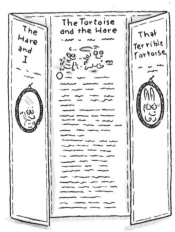

Book Link

Use *The Pain and the Great One*, by Judy Blume, to further explore the concept of point of view. In this picture book, a brother and sister each give an account of why they think Mom and Dad love the other sibling best.

3 Read together the third-person story of *The Tortoise and the Hare* (a fable by Aesop) in the middle of the mini-book. Then have students open each door to reveal how the Tortoise and the Hare might each begin an alternative version of the story. Invite students to finish each animal's account in the space provided.

Hare's Story

It's not easy being the fastest and smartest animal in the forest. I need to practice my running, but none of the other animals ever want to race me. To tell you the truth, I think they're just jealous.

One day I finally got someone to race me. It was my neighbor, Tortoise. I knew I would win. But what that trickster did to me still makes me hopping mad...

Finish the story from Hare's point of view.

‖ ‖ ‖ ‖ ‖ ‖ ‖ ‖ ‖

The Tortoise and the Hare

⊱ BY AESOP ⊰

Once upon a time,

a Tortoise and a Hare lived not far from one another in a great, green forest. Hare often bragged that he was the fastest and smartest animal in the woods.

One day Hare challenged Tortoise to a race. "We'll race from this cedar tree to the pond," Hare said. "Why not?" replied Tortoise. And as soon as Squirrel gave the signal, the two animals were off.

Hare sped past Tortoise right away. Soon he was so far ahead, he could no longer see or hear Tortoise. So Hare decided he had time to take a quick nap under a shady tree.

While Hare slept, Tortoise kept creeping along. After a while, he came upon Hare, who was still snoring. But Tortoise knew it was no time for a nap. Instead he kept going, slow and steady. Finally, he reached the pond. "You won, Tortoise!" shouted the other animals. And they threw a party to celebrate his success.

Tortoise's Story

Everyone in this forest knows I always move at the same speed—superslow. Being slow doesn't bother me. But what does bug me is my neighbor, Hare. Hare thinks he is the fastest and smartest animal in these woods. One day I got a chance to prove him wrong.

It all started when Hare challenged me to a race. I was going to say no, but then I thought, Why not? I won't win, but I can use the exercise.

Finish the story from Tortoise's point of view:

‖ ‖ ‖ ‖ ‖ ‖ ‖ ‖ ‖

That Terrible Tortoise

BY
HARE

The Hare and I

BY
TORTOISE

Exploring Dialogue

What Did They Say?

(Use with Kids' Page 36.)

Good story writers weave dialogue into their tales to subtly convey details about the plot, characters, and setting. Well-written dialogue sounds natural, not forced; in fact, readers may not even be immediately conscious of the switch from narration to dialogue. To create such natural-sounding dialogue, students should pay attention to the conversations happening all around them—at the dinner table, in the classroom, on the school yard.

Students should also carefully select which portions of their stories they will tell in dialogue format. Putting too much of a story in dialogue form can make the tale as cumbersome and boring as a court transcript. But be patient; it can take a lot of practice before young writers have a good sense of where to begin and end the dialogue in their stories.

In this activity students write dialogue for specific situations. The activity asks students to think about what characters might be thinking or feeling at a given moment and how those characters might put their thoughts into words. Be sure to remind students to use correct punctuation for their dialogue. After completing the exercise, encourage students to incorporate bits of dialogue into their own stories.

Materials

- copy of Kids' Page 36 for each student

What Did They Say?

Read each situation. Then write what each person might say. (HINT: Don't forget to put quotation marks around each person's exact words!)

1 You made your mom a special gift for Mother's Day, but now you can't find it. While you're searching, you see your dad in the kitchen.

You might say: _____

_____

Your dad might say: _____

_____

2 Jack is working in his family's vegetable garden. His next-door neighbor, Hannah, stops by.

Hannah might say: _____

_____

Jack might say: _____

_____

3 Nora stayed home from school with a cold. Her twin brother, Sam, just came home with exciting news.

Nora might say: _____

_____

Sam might say: _____

_____

4 You and your teacher are looking at a great Web site all about bears.

You might say: _____

_____

Your teacher might say: _____

_____

Building Skills in Writing: Story Writing   Scholastic Professional Books

Exploring Word Choice and Story Organization

Exploring Word Choice and Story Organization

Be Specific! Story Puzzle

(Use with Kids' Page 38.)

Readers love details, from the smells in the air as a character strolls through a carnival to the style of clothes a character wears on the first day of school. One way writers can provide such details is to choose specific words over more general ones. For example, in the classic fairy tale *The Three Bears*, we read not just that Mama Bear made *breakfast* but that she made *steaming-hot porridge*. In *Badger's Bad Mood*, by Hiawyn Oram, we read not just that Mole *helped Badger get ready for the ceremony* but that *he helped Badger press his suit and waistcoat*. Of course, illustrations also add detail to a story, but, as these examples show, word choice can make a big difference.

In this story puzzle, young writers rewrite a story sentence-by-sentence, replacing the tired, general underlined words with more specific ones. Then students have an additional challenge—to arrange the sentences in logical sequence to make a story. When they have completed the puzzle, they will have a detail-rich story to use as a model for their own writing.

To use the activity, simply have students cut out the sentence cards on the Be Specific! Story Puzzle reproducible. Students should read each sentence carefully, then flip the card over and rewrite the sentence, replacing the underlined words with more specific words. Once students have rewritten all of the sentences, they can set about putting the sentences in proper order. If you'd like, paste the finished stories onto a piece of construction paper or staple the edges of the cards to make a mini-book. Students will enjoy reading their classmates' work, since different details will give each story a slightly different twist!

Materials

- copy of Kids' Page 38 for each student
- scissors
- construction paper (optional)
- tape or stapler (optional)

When they got off the ride, they ran toward a very big fun house.

When they climbed down from the ride, they raced toward a gigantic, wacky-looking fun house.

Be Specific! Story Puzzle

Make your own exiting story. Here's how:

1. Cut out the cards. Read the sentence on each card, then turn the card over. Rewrite the sentence, replacing the underlined word with a more specific word or words. For example, instead of <u>building</u> you might write <u>silver skyscraper</u>. Instead of <u>very cold</u>, you might write <u>freezing</u>.
2. Put the cards in order to make a story.

Their first stop was the food stand, where they ate a snack.	Finally, they played a game and won a prize for their new friend.
Inside the fun house, Ryan and his dad heard something.	Then they went on a ride.
One night Ryan and his dad drove to the fair in their car.	When they got off the ride, they ran toward a very big fun house.
Ryan and his dad found the child's relatives.	It turned out to be a child who had gotten lost!

3

Bringing Stories to Life: Exploring Story Genres

In chapter 2 your students practiced developing pulse-quickening plots, creative characters, and other elements of a good story. Now they are ready to start combining those elements in the creation of their own original tales. In this chapter you'll find lessons designed to let students try their own hand at several specific story genres, including personal narratives, myths, mysteries, and adventures.

As I mentioned in chapter 1, be sure to continue reading aloud from each of these genres so that your emergent writers have authentic models to follow. I recommend having students try writing one genre at a time, preferably in connection with a story you've just read or are currently reading. For a brief description of each genre and a list of recommended books, turn to page 8.

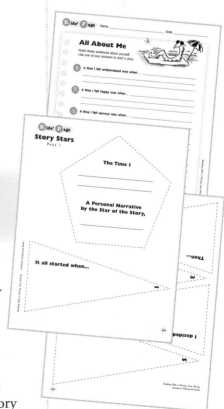

I'm the Star of the Story

WRITING SKILLS Students will brainstorm topics of personal relevance and write a personal narrative about an event from their own lives.

Personal narratives are usually the first stories we teach students to write. That's because students can come up with personal narratives simply by remembering events that have actually happened to them. They can get accustomed to the rules and wonders of storytelling, confident in the knowledge that they already know what happened first, next, and last.

While not all personal narratives are true stories, it's wise to have students start off writing about actual experiences. (We've all heard the advice, "Write what you know.") In this lesson students will first conduct a personal inventory

Materials

- copies of Kids' Pages 42–44 for each student
- scissors
- tape or glue sticks
- construction paper, for mounting the stories (optional)

to recall interesting experiences that might be worth sharing. Then they will choose a single experience and draft narratives using ready-to-go guidelines. The end result—a star-shaped story in which the student narrator is at the very center—is a visual reminder that personal narratives revolve around the experience of the author or narrator.

Prewriting

◎ Distribute the All About Me reproducible on page 42 and have students respond to each prompt. Invite them to choose one event that they remember well. This will be the topic for their star-shaped story.

◎ On a piece of scrap paper or in a journal, encourage students to brainstorm everything they remember about the experience, including how they felt at the time.

◎ Distribute the Story Stars patterns on pages 43 and 44. Have students cut out the center (the pentagon) and the five points of the star.

Writing and Revising

1 Have students complete the center of the star, which will serve as a cover or title section for their stories. They should fill in both the title of the narrative and their own name.

2 Next, direct students to draft their stories on the points of the star, starting with point number 1. Each star point includes a short prompt designed to help students navigate their narratives. They are:

> **It all started when...**
>
> **Then...**
>
> **Suddenly...**
>
> **I decided to...**
>
> **Finally...**

If you would prefer not to use the prompts, simply turn the star points over to their blank sides and have students write freehand.

3 Provide extra sets of star points, and have students revise as many times as they feel necessary.

Here's one example:

5

Finally... a piece of steak shot across the kitchen floor. Crystal was okay!

It all started when... we sat down to Sunday dinner. We were having steak and baked potatoes. Everyone was starving!

1

The Time I

Saved My

Sister's Life

A Personal Narrative by the Star of the Story,

David DiGiacamo

I decided to... help. I remembered learning the Heimlich maneuver at school. I hugged Crystal from behind and squeezed.

4

Then... my sister, Crystal, started making a funny noise. She ran away from the table. Everyone yelled, "Crystal, what's wrong?" But she didn't answer.

2

Suddenly... I realized what was happening. Crystal was choking!

3

Extending Learning

Editing and Publishing

Help students edit and proofread their work. When they're happy with their work, create final versions. Tape or paste each star point to the center of the star, with the number 1 point sitting at or near the top of the circle. If you'd like, mount the stars on construction paper or staple them to a class bulletin board titled "Our Story Stars." If students wish to elaborate further on their personal narratives, encourage them to do so on another sheet of paper.

A diary is another excellent format for exploring personal narratives. As an alternative or extension to the story-star activity, invite students to recount their experiences in "Dear Diary" form.

All About Me

Finish these sentences about yourself.
Use one of your answers to start a story.

1   **A time I felt embarrassed was when...** _____

_____

_____ .

2   **A time I felt happy was when...** _____

_____

_____ .

3   **A time I felt nervous was when...** _____

_____

_____ .

4   **I learned something new when...** _____

_____

_____ .

5   **A time I helped someone or someone helped me was...** _____

_____

_____ .

6   **One of my favorite vacations was...** _____

_____

_____ .

7   **Once I found a...** _____

_____

_____ .

The Time I

_____

_____

**A Personal Narrative
by the Star of the Story,**

_____

It all started when...

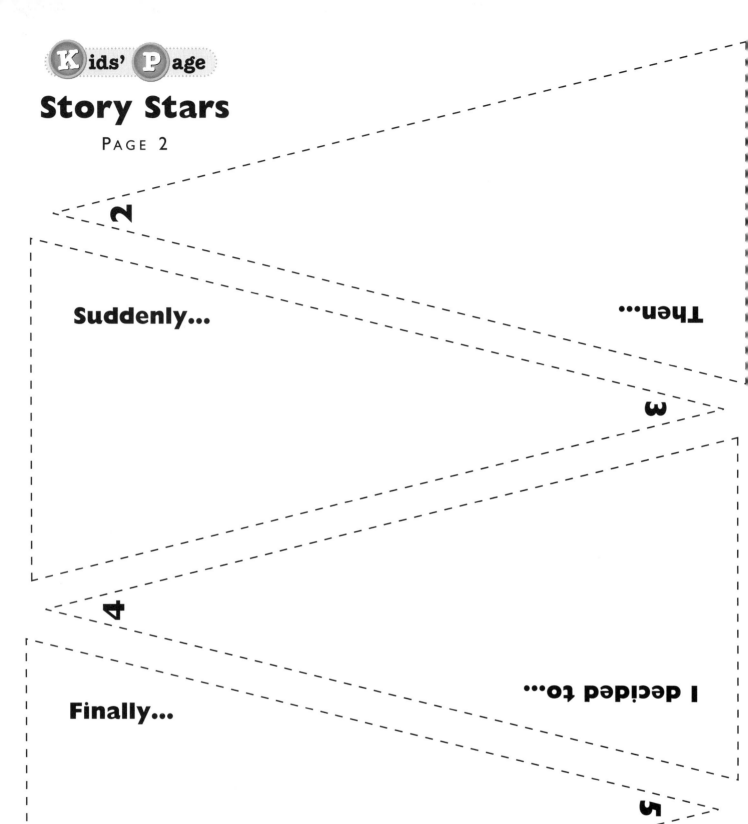

2

Suddenly...

Then...

3

4

I decided to...

Finally...

5

Building Skills in Writing: Story Writing
Scholastic Professional Books

Be a Mythmaker

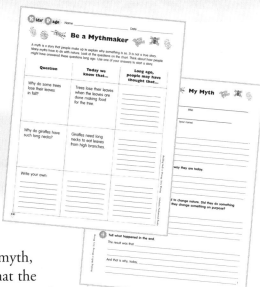

WRITING SKILLS Students will write their own pourquoi, or "why," stories, providing explanations of natural occurrences that are rooted in imagination rather than science.

Prewriting

◎ Read aloud an example of a myth (see below). Explain that, in a myth, animals might talk and take on specific personalities. Point out that the characters in a myth often do something that will forever change a part of the world, so that the story takes on a three-part structure:

> **Back then, things were like this…**
> **But then this happened…**
> **That's why things are now like this…**

◎ Distribute the Be a Mythmaker grid on page 46 and invite students to fill in possible creative explanations for each of the natural occurrences.

Writing and Revising

Have students use page 47 to develop one of their ideas into a full-fledged myth. The My Myth reproducible provides a general structure that students may follow, but they need not feel limited to this format.

Editing and Publishing

◎ Have students edit and proofread their stories. For their final versions, have them spread the stories out over several pages and add artwork. Then pair each writer with a younger student at your school and let them read the myth together.

◎ Graph how many students chose to write about each "why" question. Then have several students who wrote on the same topic read aloud their stories to demonstrate the amazing places our imagination can take us.

Materials

● copies of Kids' Pages 46 and 47 for each student

A Myth to Share

A long time ago, in the African wilderness, the animals were sad because their friend Ant had died. To honor Ant, the animals had a procession. They marched, sang, and played the drums.

Now, back then, Leopard had a beautiful golden coat without a single spot. But that would soon change—all because of Leopard's greediness.

On the day of the procession, Leopard was finding it hard to sing along with the other animals. He was too hungry! When he saw that a farmer had left out some eggs, Leopard ate every last one!

The farmer was furious. He wanted to catch the animal that had stolen his eggs. So he built a fire and called the animals over. "I want each of you to leap over the fire," the farmer said. "The one whose belly is full of my eggs will fall in."

One by one, the animals jumped over the fire. Then it was Leopard's turn. He was determined to fool the farmer, so he jumped very high. But alas, he fell right back down into the flames. The fire burned black spots into his beautiful coat. And that is why Leopard has spots to this very day.

Be a Mythmaker

A myth is a story that people make up to explain why something is so. It is not a true story. Many myths have to do with nature. Look at the questions on the chart. Think about how people might have answered these questions long ago. Use one of your answers to start a story.

Question	Today we know that...	Long ago, people may have thought that...
Why do some trees lose their leaves in fall?	Trees lose their leaves when the leaves are done making food for the tree.	_____ _____ _____ _____ _____ _____ _____
Why do giraffes have such long necks?	Giraffes need long necks to eat leaves from high branches.	_____ _____ _____ _____ _____ _____ _____
Write your own: _____ _____ _____ _____	_____ _____ _____ _____	_____ _____ _____ _____

Building Skills in Writing: Story Writing   Scholastic Professional Books

Why _____
(title)

by _____
(your name)

1 **Describe the setting and characters.**

Long ago, in _____ ,

there lived _____

_____

and _____

_____ .

2 **Tell how things were different from the way they are today.**

Back then, _____

_____

_____

_____ .

3 **Tell what the character or characters did to change nature. Did they do something selfish and get punished by others? Did they change something on purpose? Use your imagination!**

One day, _____

_____

_____

_____ .

4 **Tell what happened in the end.**

The result was that _____

_____

_____ .

And that is why, today, _____

_____

_____ !

Adventure Awaits

WRITING SKILLS Using a comic-book format, students will create adventure stories with action-packed plots and dialogue.

Materials

- copies of Kids' Pages 50 and 51 for each student
- scissors
- stapler
- markers

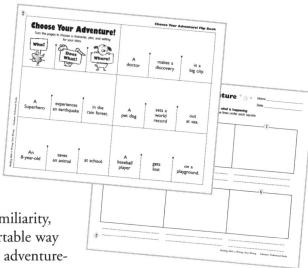

Did you ever catch a student reading a comic book when he or she was supposed to be doing something else? For many children, there is something irresistible about the comic format. The dramatic pictures and vivid dialogue help them visualize the story, and comic plots are usually full of twists and turns. Because of this appeal and familiarity, the comic-book concept is a comfortable way for students to try their hand at the adventure-story genre.

Prewriting

◉ Have fun brainstorming adventure plots! One way to come up with ideas is to make and use the Choose Your Adventure! flip book on page 50.

1 Make copies of the reproducible and instruct students to cut out the six rectangles along the outer dotted lines.

2 Then, have students cut along the vertical dotted lines on each rectangle.

3 Direct students to stack the rectangles together, placing the one with the heading *Who?*, *Does What?*, *Where?* on top, and staple along the top edge.

4 Finally, have students flip through the three sections until they find a Character-Plot-

Setting combination they like. Of course, they can add other characters and situations to their adventure stories. Examples of possible adventure-story concepts from the flip book include a pet dog who gets lost out at sea, an 8-year-old who sets a world record on a playground, a Superhero who saves an animal in the rain forest, and dozens more.

Writing and Revising

1 Once students have selected topics for their adventure stories, distribute the My Comic Adventure reproducible on page 51. Offer some examples of the different kinds of writing in a comic book. Point out that dialogue normally goes in speech balloons, and a character's private thoughts go in thought balloons. A summary of the action is often placed at the bottom of the frame.

2 Invite students to draft their comic adventures in pencil. They should wait until they have revised and polished their work before creating a final version with colored markers.

(NOTE: Point out to students that they need not fill the whole page, and they may use more than one page if they'd like. Make multiple copies of the reproducible available.)

Editing and Publishing

Students can edit each other's work using the Editing My Story checklist on page 62. As a publishing option, consider binding everyone's adventure comics in a homemade book and sending a copy home to each family. If you aren't able to make color copies, even black-and-white versions of the adventures are sure to "wow" parents and friends!

Choose Your Adventure!

Turn the pages to choose a character, plot, and setting for your story.

Who?

Does What?

Where?

Who?	Does What?	Where?
A doctor	makes a discovery	in a big city.
A pet dog	sets a world record	out at sea.
A baseball player	gets lost	on a playground.
A Superhero	experiences an earthquake	in the rain forest.
An 8-year-old	saves an animal	at school.

Date _____

☆ ★ My Comic Adventure ★ ☆

Kids' Page

◎ Draw a ⬭ to show what someone **says**.

◎ Draw a ⬭ₒₒₒ to show what someone **thinks**.

◎ Write **what is happening** on the lines under each square.

① ② ③

④ ⑤ ⑥

Crack the Case!

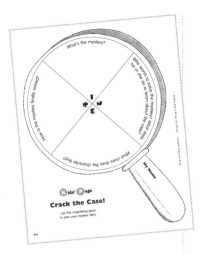

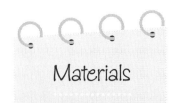

Materials

● copy of Kids'
Page 54 for each
student

WRITING SKILLS Students will write original mysteries featuring puzzling
situations, clues, suspense, and satisfying resolutions.

My love of mysteries began in second and third grade, when I was rarely
seen without a yellow-bound Nancy Drew book in my hands. For me as
for many readers, the attraction comes from the way in which a mystery writer
invites the reader into the tale, leaving important clues for the reader to find
along the way. Of course, creating this sort of story is far from easy: The writer
must know just how much information to give away and just how much to
withhold. He or she must also end the story in a way that seems plausible and
satisfying.

In this activity your students learn the craft of mystery writing by using a
ready-to-go mystery organizer. They'll come up with a mystery to solve, a
character to solve it, some clues, and a solid ending.

Prewriting

◎ Distribute the Crack the Case! reproducible on page 54 and ask if anyone
can name the tool pictured on the page (*a magnifying glass*). Discuss why a
magnifying glass might be used as a symbol of mysteries. (*In old-fashioned
mysteries, detectives would use these magnifying glasses to search for fingerprints
and other clues.*)

◎ Point out and discuss the different sections of the magnifying glass.

Writing and Revising

Have students come up with concepts and titles for their mysteries. One fun
way to do this is to have each student begin by writing "The Case of the
_____ _____" on a sheet of paper. Then, on the
board, list these two columns of words:

Column A	Column B
Disappearing	Shoes
Noisy	Backpack
Shrinking	Dog
Mixed-Up	Flowers
Grouchy	Neighbor
Dirty	Footprints
Missing	Snowman
Broken	Computer
Forgotten	Birthday Cake
Giant	Mittens

Have each student select one word from column A to place in the first blank, and one word from column B to place in the second. Voila—a mystery title!

2 Once they've settled on a title, have students begin drafting their stories on the magnifying glass-shaped organizer. Remind students that this organizer is simply a way to create an outline of a story and that they'll need to elaborate and revise several times before their mysteries are ready for publishing.

Editing and Publishing

Have students edit their mysteries using the Editing My Story checklist on page 62. Publish the stories by having each student read his or her tale aloud at a special "mystery party." Set the mood by having students sit in a circle around a pretend campfire. Serve marshmallows for a storytime snack, and have students provide sound effects for the tales.

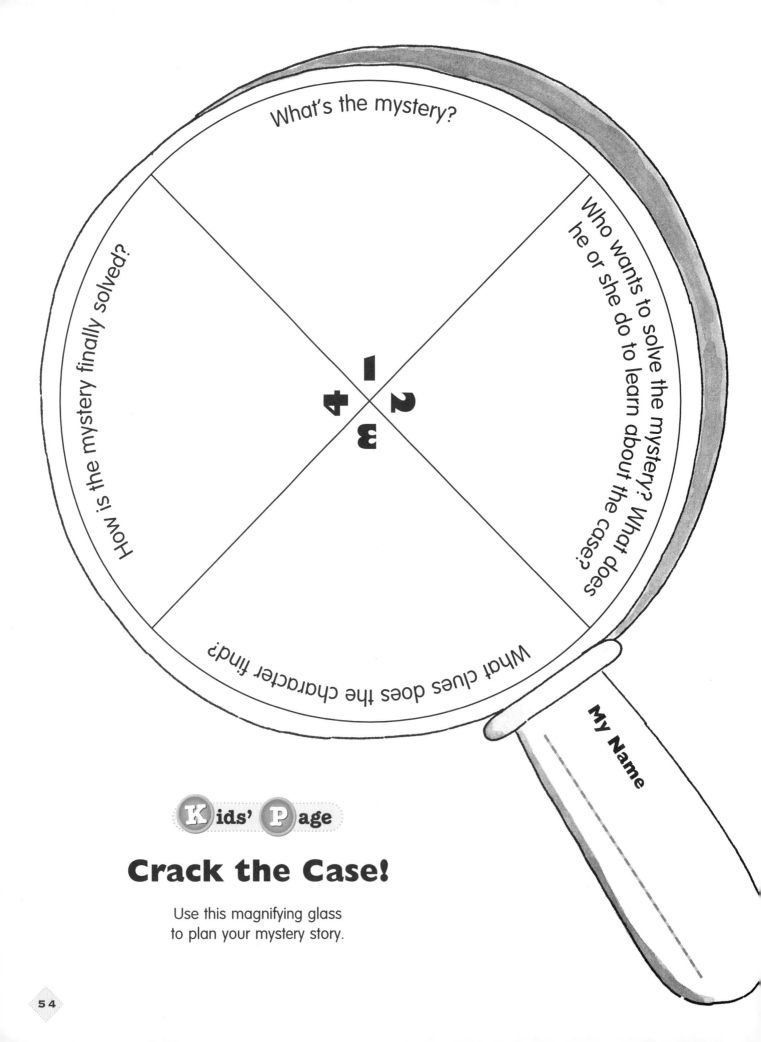

What's the mystery?

Who wants to solve the mystery? What does he or she do to learn about the case?

How is the mystery finally solved?

What clues does the character find?

1
2
3
4

My Name

Kids' **P**age

Crack the Case!

Use this magnifying glass to plan your mystery story.

Additional Ideas for Exploring Different Genres

The following activities will help you teach students to write historical fiction, tall tales, fantasies and fairy tales, and humorous stories.

Historical Fiction

(Use with Kids' Page 58.)

If you and your students read historical fiction together, you already know that it's a wonderful way to shine light on a specific time and place in history. A quality work of historical fiction is full of delicious details: what people wore, what they ate, how they worked and played, how they spoke, and so on. Writing one's own historical-fiction story is the perfect way to explore how authors weave together such facts with fiction to make a seamless narrative.

Help students get started writing historical fiction by distributing the All Aboard the Time Machine! reproducible on page 58. It will help students collect the rich details that make historical fiction interesting. When students are finished their Time Machine "excursions," have them use their research to craft a short piece of historical fiction.

Tall Tales

Unlike historical fiction and modern realistic fiction, the details in a tall tale need not be plausible. In fact, the more outrageous the descriptions, the better! Here's your students' chance to create characters that are strong enough to dig the Grand Canyon, big enough to walk from continent to continent, or whatever else kids' imaginations dictate.

To launch a tall-tale-writing project, read aloud several examples of tall tales and discuss the use of exaggeration. Together, practice using concrete terms to describe a person or character. For example, name a popular sports star (or other well-known person) and have kids offer adjectives describing him or her. When students say, "fast," ask, "How fast is she?" When students say, "tall," ask, "How tall is he?" Encourage students to use their imaginations, and you'll come up with some descriptions worthy of tall tales:

◎ *Shaquille O'Neil is so tall, he has to duck to avoid airplanes.*

◎ *Our principal is so smart, she was doing math problems the day she was born.*

◎ *My grandpa is so strong, he brings his house with him when he comes to visit us.*

Finally, have students try drafting their own tall tales. For a "tall" publishing format, cut several sheets of posterboard into long, four-inch-wide strips and

Materials

● copies of Kids' Page 58 for each student

have students write their tall tales on these. If students would like some guidance, offer the following sequential prompts:

1 This is the story of _____ , the _____ man/woman who ever lived. *(Students fill in the second blank with a superlative adjective such as strongest, smallest, tallest, wildest, etc.)*

2 _____ 's parents first knew he/she was going to be _____ when _____ . *(Students give an exaggerated anecdote from the character's childhood.)*

3 When _____ grew up, he/she was so _____ , he/she could _____ .

4 He/she could even _____ and _____ . *(In both 3 and 4, students give concrete examples of the larger-than-life things the character could do.)*

5 But most of all, people are still talking about the time he/she _____ . *(Students narrate the main event of the story in detail. It can be a contest, challenge, act of heroism, etc.)*

Fantasy and Fairy Tales

(Use with Kids' Page 59.)

Introduce the fantasy genre with some classic fairy tales, then have students write fairy tales of their own. Before kids begin writing, brainstorm some of the common elements found in fairy tales. For example, many fairy tales follow a simple formula:

◎ There is a likeable hero or heroine. He or she may be rich or poor.

◎ The hero or heroine has a dream or problem. For example, Cinderella wants desperately to get to the ball. Snow White needs to escape from the wicked queen.

◎ Something fantastic (magical or out of this world) happens to allow the character to solve the problem or attain the dream. For example, it might be a wish granted by a genie or a magical kiss.

Help students get their creative juices going by offering story starters in the form of "magic beans."

1 Make a copy of the Magic Beans reproducible on page 59 for each student.

2 Have students cut out the beans and put them in three envelopes (Heroes and Heroines, Other Characters, Situations).

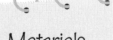

Materials

● copies of Kids' Page 59 for each student
● scissors
● three envelopes for each student

3 Then, instruct each student to randomly draw one bean from each of his or her envelopes and use those story elements in an original fairy tale. (Allow one opportunity for students to re-draw if they'd like.) Of course, students can add additional characters and situations to their stories.

4 Invite students to return to their envelopes and repeat step 3 whenever they need to jumpstart a fairy tale.

Humor

Just what makes a story funny? Ask your students, and you'll probably find that they have a hard time answering. For most of us, humor is easily recognized but not so easily defined.

When you set out to explore the humor genre with your students, look for some common characteristics in the funny books you have shared together. You will find that humorous stories often:

◎ Turn an everyday situation topsy-turvy. For example, in *Gregory, the Terrible Eater*, by Mitchell Sharmat, Gregory's parents take him to see Dr. Ram because he is not eating properly. Sounds like a situation any kid might find himself in—except Gregory is a goat who prefers eggs and fruit over shoes and tin cans! And in the Caldecott Honor Book *Click, Clack, Moo: Cows That Type*, by Doreen Cronin, readers find out what happens when some contentious farm animals learn to type.

◎ Poke fun at the small mishaps and embarrassing situations we all face. For example, in *Dog Breath*, by Dav Pilkey, readers laugh at the havoc poor Halitosis wreaks with his doggy breath, then delight when he uses his bad breath to save the day.

Your students may find a few other common denominators as well, such as the use of puns and plays on words. When they're ready to try writing their own funny tales, encourage them with some of the "What If?" prompts listed at right. Students can use the prompts as is or adapt them to create an entirely original story.

What If?

◎ You and your pet switched bodies for the day?

◎ You ripped your pants in the middle of gym class?

◎ A squirrel became President?

◎ A dog really did eat your homework but no one believed you?

◎ You had a strange new babysitter?

◎ You and a friend got locked in a grocery store overnight?

◎ You moved into a new house and everything began to go wrong?

Name _____   Date _____

All Aboard the Time Machine!

Are you writing a story about the past? You will need lots of details. Use this "time machine" to travel back in time. You can use books and other resources to answer the questions. Later, use your answers to write your historical story.

YEAR

Start!

I want my story to happen in

_____

in the year

_____

What did people wear back then?

_____

_____

What were some popular foods?

_____

_____

What important events were happening?

_____

_____

What jobs did people have?

_____

_____

What did people do for fun?

_____

_____

Finish!

Now you are ready to write your story!

Magic Beans

Make your own exciting fairy tale. Here's how:

1. Cut out the "beans" and place them in three envelopes: Heroes and Heroines, Other Characters, and Situations.

2. Pick one bean from each envelope to start a fabulous fairy tale!

Heroes and Heroines	Other Characters	Situations
Princess	Fairy godmother	A secret spell
Prince	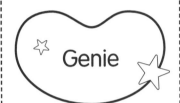Genie	Three wishes
Servant girl	Elf	A special cape
Farmer	Talking frog	A magic kiss
Brave knight	Shepherd	A magic wand
Mermaid	Mysterious guest	A riddle to solve

Building Skills in Writing: Story Writing Scholastic Professional Books

Wrapping Up Stories: Suggestions for Editing, Publishing, and Assessing

Many specific tips for editing, publishing, and assessing students' stories are found in the preceding chapters. The following are some additional general suggestions, checklists, and rubrics to assist you and your students in the final stages of the story-writing process.

Editing

Before students hand in their stories, have them work with partners to edit and polish their work. Distribute copies of the Editing My Story checklist on page 62 for students to use as they edit their own and each other's stories. Student writers should hand in a copy of this checklist along with their final stories to show that they have completed the self-editing and peer-editing processes.

Because students probably have little experience in editing other people's work, you might want to take a few minutes for a crash course in respectful editing. Invite students to brainstorm things they think an editor should and should not do, and develop a list of rules for your classroom. For example, you will need to decide as a class whether editors will write directly on the original writer's story. If so, they should use pencil just in case the edits are incorrect. At the top of your list of rules for editors, be sure to include the following basics:

◉ **Be Positive** Point out the best parts of your partner's story.

◉ **Be Specific** Show the writer exactly which words or parts you have questions about.

◉ **Be Polite** Don't use words like *dumb* or *bad*.

◉ **Keep It Private** Don't share comments about your partner's work with anyone but him or her.

To streamline the editing process, provide students with a copy of the editing symbols on page 63.

Publishing

For many children, publishing is the stage of the writing process that makes it all worthwhile. Knowing that a real audience will read their stories is the force that motivates them through the other necessary stages—prewriting, drafting, revising, and editing. Keep in mind that there are countless ways to publish students' stories. You'll find some suggestions at the end of each writing lesson in chapter 3. Other ideas include:

◎ Deliver students' illustrated stories to a nursing home or children's hospital. If possible, have students make the trip and read their stories to residents/patients.

◎ Compile students' best stories in a semiannual literary magazine that gets distributed to parents and others in the school community. Simply make black-and-white copies of the stories and staple them together. Have students vote on a title and design a cover.

◎ Have students bind their stories with construction paper (cover with contact paper for durability) and string. Place the homemade books in the school library for other students to borrow.

◎ Have young writers seek publication in a "real" children's magazine or Web site. Be sure to check out the publication's guidelines for submissions before sending students' work. For example, many magazines require that stories be typed neatly and include the writer's name and address on each page. Guidelines are usually available by writing to the editor or checking the Web site. I've included a short list of resources at right.

Assessment

Before students begin a story-writing project, define your criteria for evaluating the work. To determine how well students have met your criteria, use a rubric—a scale that allows you to assign a score to each facet of a student's work. On page 64, you'll find a rubric designed to help you assess content, mechanics, and presentation in nearly any story. You may copy and use the rubric as is or adapt it to suit your individual needs. You can also provide copies to students so that they can evaluate their own stories. Afterward, meet with each student to discuss your evaluation of his or her story and to provide suggestions for improving the story.

You'll be amazed at how students' story-writing abilities grow and develop over the course of the year. Record that progress by having students keep portfolios of their writing. You should work with each student to select the pieces that will go into the portfolio. Look not only for stories that exemplify the student's best work but also for those that show improvement or a willingness to take risks and try new skills (for example, the first time the student includes dialogue in a story). Parents will enjoy browsing through their child's writing portfolio at conference time, and you'll have an ongoing testament to each student's progress.

Who Publishes Children's Stories?

Magazines

◎ *New Moon,* P.O. Box 3620, Duluth, MN 55806. Go to www.newmoon.org for guidelines.

◎ *Highlights for Children,* 803 Church Street, Honesdale, PA 18431

◎ *Stone Soup: The Magazine for Children,* P.O. Box 83, Santa Cruz, CA 95063

Web sites

◎ Log on to www.cyberkids.com/CyberKids.html to publish students' stories, articles, poetry, puzzles, and art. Click on Welcome for submission guidelines.

◎ Go to http://kids.mysterynet.com/ for a monthly "Mysteries by Kids" contest.

Name _____ Date _____

Editing My Story

Before you hand in your story, work with a partner to make sure it is in tip-top shape. Put a ✔ next to each item after you check it. Ask your partner to do the same.

	I checked.	Partner checked.
The story has interesting characters.	◯	◯
The story has a clear setting.	◯	◯
The story has a plot with a beginning, middle, and ending.	◯	◯
It's easy to understand the point of view (who's telling the story).	◯	◯
Ideas in the story are in an order that makes sense.	◯	◯
The sentences in the story don't all start the same way.	◯	◯
The sentences end in periods, question marks, or exclamation points.	◯	◯
Paragraphs are indented.	◯	◯
Commas are used when needed.	◯	◯
Quotation marks are used when needed.	◯	◯
Other punctuation is used correctly.	◯	◯
Words in the story are spelled correctly.	◯	◯

Name _____ Date _____

Editing Symbols

Use these symbols when you edit your own writing and your classmates' writing.

Symbol	It Means	Example
☰	Use a capital letter.	Atlanta, georgia ☰
/	Use a lowercase letter.	I like chocolate /Cake.
∧	Insert (add) something.	Colin is ᵐʸ∧brother.
ℓ	Remove something.	It is ~~very~~ very hot.
⊙	Add a period.	The rain fell ⊙
↗	Add a comma.	I have dogs ↗cats, and fish.
¶	Indent for a new paragraph.	¶ Later that day, Marcie heard a noise.
∼	Transpose (switch position).	Th⁀ie⁀r house is nearby.

Story Feedback Sheet

Use this rubric to assess students' stories.

Student's Name _____

Title of Story _____

Genre _____

		Outstanding	Good	Needs Work
Story Content	Setting	____	____	____
	Characters	____	____	____
	Plot	____	____	____
	Dialogue	____	____	____
	Organization	____	____	____
	Point of view	____	____	____
	Word choice	____	____	____
	Other:			
	_____	____	____	____
Grammar/ Mechanics	Complete sentences	____	____	____
	Correct spelling	____	____	____
	Correct use of terminal punctuation	____	____	____
	Correct use of commas	____	____	____
	Correct use of quotation marks	____	____	____
	Other:			
	_____	____	____	____
Presentation/ Publishing	Neatness	____	____	____
	Illustrations	____	____	____
	Other:			
	_____	____	____	____

My favorite part of your story is _____

_____ .

One way you could make your story even better is _____

_____ .